SWEPT AWAY

The Story of
the 2011 Japanese Tsunami

BY REBECCA RISSMAN

Consultant:
Michael Wert, PhD
Associate Professor of History
Marquette University, Milwaukee

CAPSTONE PRESS
a capstone imprint

Tangled History is published by Capstone Press,
1710 Roe Crest Drive, North Mankato, Minnesota 56003
www.mycapstone.com

Library of Congress Cataloging-in-Publication Data
Names: Rissman, Rebecca, author.
Title: Swept away : the story of the 2011 Japanese tsunami / by Rebecca Rissman.
Other titles: Tangled history.
Description: North Mankato, Minnesota : Capstone Press, [2017] |
Series: Tangled history | Audience: Ages 9-14. | Audience: Grades 4 to 6. |
Includes bibliographical references.
Identifiers: LCCN 2016038584
ISBN 9781515736059 (library binding)
ISBN 9781515736097 (pbk.)
ISBN 9781515736332 (ebook (pdf)
Subjects: LCSH: Tohoku Earthquake and Tsunami, Japan, 2011—Juvenile literature.
| Tsunamis—Japan—Juvenile literature. | Fukushima Nuclear Disaster, Japan,
2011—Juvenile literature. | Natural disasters—Japan—Juvenile literature. | Japan—
History—21st century—Juvenile literature.
Classification: LCC QE537.2.J3 R57 2017 | DDC 363.34/940952—dc23
LC record available at https://lccn.loc.gov/2016038584

Editorial Credits
Adrian Vigliano, editor; Kyle Grenz, designer; Tracy Cummins, media researcher;
Laura Manthe, production specialist

Photo Credits
Alamy: epa european pressphoto agency b.v., 22, TEPCO, 7, Zuma Press/Tokyo Electric Power Company/J,
17; Dreamstime: Aduldej Sukaram, 92; Getty Images: Athit Perawongmetha, 70, Gamma-Rapho, 19, HIROSHI
KAWAHARA/AFP, 31, JIJI PRESS/AFP, 100, Kurita KAKU, 34, Kyodo News, 37, 88, 97, Pallava Bagla, 72,
SADATSUGU TOMIZAWA/AFP, 20, Sankei, 15, 53, The Asahi Shimbun, Cover, Tomohiro Ohsumi/Bloomberg,
8, 54; iStockphoto: Andrea Zanchi, 26, ArtwayPics, 78, 91; Newscom: ABACA, 48, Abaca France/ABACAUSA.
COM, 77, Air Photo Service/ABACAUSA.COM, 44, EPA/DAVID GUTTENFELDER, 60, MC3 Kyle Carlstrom/
NVNS/ABACAUSA.COM, 105; Reuters: Yuriko Nakao, 83; Shutterstock: april70, Cover Background;
Thinkstock: LaChouettePhoto, 4, Stocktrek Images, 66, 84

Printed in the United States of America.
10063S17

TABLE OF CONTENTS

Foreword.. 4
1 An Earthquake Strikes.. 8
2 A Wall of Water... 20
3 The Tsunami Rolls In.. 26
4 A Sea of Destruction... 34
5 Finding Solutions 44
6 Meltdown... 54
7 A Crisis Unfolds... 66
8 Struggling to Survive.. 72
9 Pleading for Help.. 78
10 Aftermath... 84
11 Picking Up the Pieces.. 92

Epilogue 98
Timeline... 106
Glossary 108
Critical Thinking Using the Common Core............................. 109
Internet Sites 109
Further Reading.. 110
Selected Bibliography.. 111
Index.. 112
About the Author 112

FOREWORD

nurenu saki no kasa
(It is best to have your umbrella before the rain falls)
—*Japanese Proverb*

Masao Yoshida

Fukushima Dai-Ichi Nuclear Power Plant, March 2008

Masao Yoshida grumbled as he sat down in the conference room. The square-jawed plant manager ran the sprawling seaside Fukushima Dai-Ichi nuclear plant. The plant was located on the northeastern coast of the main island of Japan, Honshu. The workers at Fukushima Dai-Ichi and 53 other nuclear plants worked hard to provide 30 percent of Japan's power. Yoshida had lots of work to do and didn't appreciate being hastily called into a meeting in the middle of the day. He joined a group of serious, quiet men in their 50s and 60s around a conference table and waited for the meeting to begin. Some wore tailored business suits. Others wore the company's crisp blue jumpsuits.

Yoshida soon learned the reason for the meeting: an internal group of scientists had released a new report in which they argued that Fukushima Dai-Ichi needed better protection against enormous ocean waves called tsunamis. A giant earthquake, they warned, could trigger a tsunami that could overwhelm the plant.

This news was irritating, but not altogether surprising. The plant had already been rebuilt once to boost its tsunami protection. A thick concrete seawall blocked the plant from the ocean's tall waves. When Fukushima Dai-Ichi was built, this wall stood about 10 feet tall. In 2002, scientists warned that it was too short. Fukushima leadership heeded the warning and rebuilt it to stand nearly 19 feet tall. But now, Yoshida saw, this new report was advising that the wall needed to be rebuilt again, to a staggering height of almost 50 feet!

It wasn't that Yoshida was unafraid of tsunamis. Far from it. He and the other managers present that day understood that tsunamis were a constant threat. As they drove into work, some had even passed tsunami markers.

Now, as Yoshida and his colleagues took in the report's details, they began to discuss the new information.

"Is this pressing?" one asked.

"How promptly should we take this up?" asked another.

The conversation continued like this for a short time, until the group eventually agreed to review the matter further at a later date.

Yoshida sighed as he stood up to leave the meeting. He wasn't worried. It certainly didn't seem likely to him that a 50-foot tsunami would happen anytime soon.

Fukushima Dai-Ichi, 2007

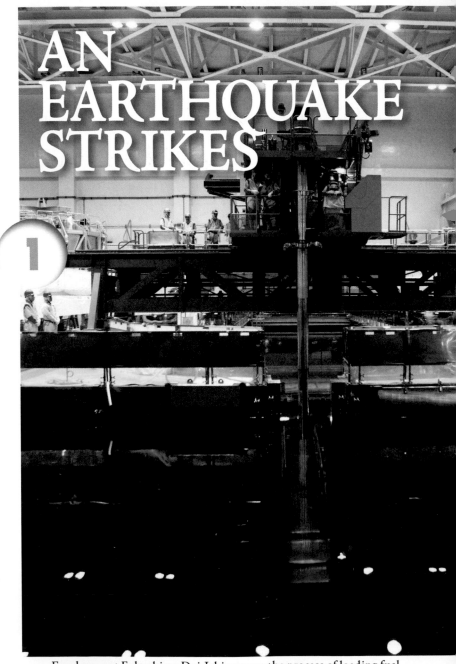

AN EARTHQUAKE STRIKES

1

Employees at Fukushima Dai-Ichi oversee the process of loading fuel into nuclear reactor 3.

Atsufumi Yoshizawa walked quickly down a long, gleaming corridor. It was almost the end of his shift. Nearly every corner of the sprawling Fukushima Dai-Ichi nuclear plant was clean and orderly, just as he liked it. Yoshizawa mentally reviewed everything he still needed to finish. He had spent the day supervising a routine shutdown of nuclear reactors 5 and 6, and he wanted to be sure everything was in order before he drove home.

Yoshizawa was an important figure at Fukushima Dai-Ichi. He was quiet and shy, but his 30 years at the plant had given him the confidence and expertise to supervise large crews of workers. He knew the inner workings of Fukushima Dai-Ichi by heart. He had spent the majority of his adult life monitoring the way the plant utilized a process called nuclear fission to heat giant pools of water. When the water got hot enough, steam was created and used to turn turbines. The plant used these turbines to create electricity. The process, he knew, seemed extraordinarily complex. But to him, it was familiar and safe and simple.

Yoshizawa had often watched the scientists who controlled the plant's nuclear fission. He knew where they stored rods of enriched uranium, the plant's very powerful and dangerous radioactive fuel. He loved observing them as they bundled rods of enriched uranium together, and then lowered them into water in a pressurized container. These bundles would instantly begin to heat the water and create steam.

In order to keep the bundles from overheating, the scientists would use materials called control rods to slow the nuclear fission process. If they needed to reduce the temperature of the water, they simply lowered the control rods farther into the uranium bundles to slow the rate of the nuclear reactions, and therefore reduce the temperature of the bundles. When they wanted to increase the temperature of the water, they simply removed the control rods from the bundles.

Everyone at the plant worked hard to make safety a high priority. Each of the Fukushima Dai-Ichi employees understood that nuclear fission releases large amounts of radiation that must be contained. All employees were well educated on the subject of radiation energy and how it can travel through other materials. In small amounts, they learned, it is harmless to living things. People are exposed to small amounts of radiation on a daily basis through X-rays and microwaves. But high doses of radiation can be very harmful, or even lethal.

And of course, the workers at Fukushima Dai-Ichi knew that the plant produced enormous quantities of radiation. It had six separate nuclear reactors to house the nuclear fission process. Each of these was built to keep the radioactive materials safely contained. The reactors were encased within layers of steel and concrete. These barriers were designed to keep radioactive solids, liquids, and gasses contained.

Without warning, violent shaking knocked Yoshizawa to his hands and knees. The walls and floor began to buck wildly as the sounds of shattering glass and falling objects rang around him. It was an earthquake. A big one. Frantically, Yoshizawa looked around for something to hide under. There was nothing in the hallway, so he crawled desperately into a nearby room and found shelter beneath a desk. Factory workers were scrambling to find protection. Someone screamed. A huge ceiling tile exploded on the ground just in front of Yoshizawa.

He looked out a window and saw something bizarre. The cars parked outside were actually bouncing up and down off the ground. Yoshizawa couldn't believe his eyes. He had lived though hundreds of earthquakes, but none had been like this. It seemed like the earthquake went on forever. Yoshizawa thought about his wife and daughter. Thankfully they were at home in Yokohama, just south of Tokyo. He hoped they were far enough away to be safe.

Just then, he was plunged into darkness. The plant had lost power.

In the dark, Yoshizawa could hear his colleagues checking on one another. A few seemed to be crying.

Despite the strength of the quake, Yoshizawa wasn't concerned about the plant; it was designed to withstand earthquakes. He knew that Toyko Electic Power Company (TEPCO), the owners of the plant, had spent tens of billions of yen implementing additional safety measures for Fukushima Dai-Ichi. There was a huge earthquake-proof control room that could be used to operate the essential functions of the plant. There was a seawall protecting the plant from any waves that might follow an earthquake. There was even an elaborate backup system in place to keep the nuclear fuel cool in the event of a power loss. Yoshizawa was confident that the Fukushima Dai-Ichi plant was a very safe place to be.

Katsunobu Sakurai

Katsunobu Sakurai, mayor of Minamisoma, was in the middle of a busy day at work. The energetic mayor had already led a meeting with his staff, and then given a speech to hundreds of schoolchildren at their graduation ceremony. He was in the middle of guiding a handful of local delegates on a tour of the fourth floor of the building when he felt the first tremble. Suddenly, the small rumblings exploded into giant, violent waves that rocked the 40-year-old building.

The mayor fell to the ground. He could hear shouts of *"tasukete!"* (help!) and *"tometekure!"* (please stop!) from the floors below. A woman shrieked. He heard crashing as office supplies fell from shelves and hit the floor.

Sakurai felt strangely calm. He looked at the swaying ceiling and wondered if it would crumble

Tokyo railway passengers react as earthquake
tremors interrupt their commute.

above him. His mantra "what will be will be" floated through his mind, as though on a gentle stream. He watched a jug of water on a nearby table as it wobbled back and forth. Just before it tipped, he reached out and caught it.

Atsufumi Yoshizawa
Control Room, Fukushima Dai-Ichi,
March 11, 2011, 2:55 p.m.

As soon as the rumblings of the earthquake stopped, Yoshizawa hurried to the plant's earthquake-safe control room. He opened the door to the windowless room and noticed that several other managers had already arrived, including Yoshida Masao, the plant's manager. Everyone inside was busy assessing the status of the nuclear plant. Yoshizawa was relieved to see that all systems were functioning as intended.

Plant managers monitor the operations of Fukushima Dai-Ichi
from inside the plant's control room.

As soon as Fukushima Dai-Ichi lost power, the plant's nuclear reactors instantly shut down. This safety precaution prevented the reactors from operating out of control. At the same time, a series of diesel backup generators had kicked in. These generators were busily powering the systems that kept the hot fuel in the nuclear reactors cool. Together, these protective measures were working to prevent a nuclear meltdown. A nuclear meltdown could happen if the nuclear fuel became so hot that it damaged the structure of the reactor and released radiation into the surrounding area.

As soon as Yoshizawa was assured that the plant was under control, he and the other managers began to account for all of their workers to learn if anyone had been injured in the quake. They also started to assess the damaged areas that needed attention immediately.

In the midst of the hubbub, Yoshizawa's mind briefly wandered to the other nuclear plants in the area: Fukushima Dai-ni, Tohoku's Onagawa, and the Tokai plant. He hoped they were all faring as well as Fukushima Dai-Ichi.

Office workers in Tokyo watch as smoke rises on the horizon following the earthquake.

A WALL OF WATER

2

Susumu Sugawara

Oshima, Japan,
March 11, 2011, 3:00 p.m.

When the earth stopped its violent
rumbles, Susumu Sugawara warily stood
up and looked around. Dozens of buildings
in his tiny island home of Oshima had
crumbled under the force of the giant
quake. Soon, the sound of the tsunami
warning siren began to wail. All around
him, surviving residents of Oshima were
hurrying to pack bags and flee to the hills.
They knew that their tiny island home was
terribly vulnerable to tsunami waves.

Sugawara loved the people of his island.
This was his home, and they were like his
family. But he didn't join them in their
flight for higher ground. Instead, he did the
unthinkable: he sprinted downhill, directly
toward the sea.

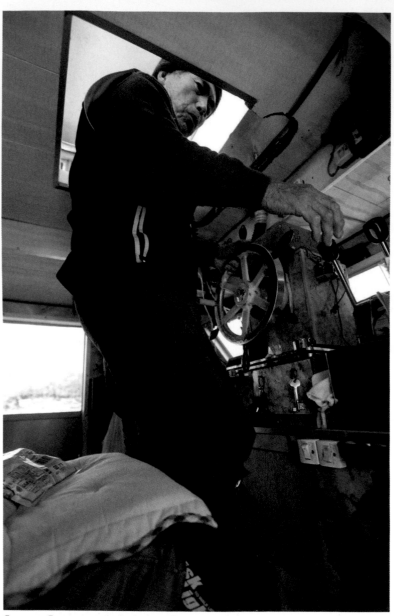

Susumu Sugawara, at the helm of his
boat, *Sunflower*

He charged down onto the dock, running as fast as his 64-year-old legs would carry him. His boat, *Sunflower*, bobbed peacefully in the sea. If it weren't for the blaring of the tsunami siren and crumbled concrete near the dock, Sugawara could have mistaken the scene for another normal day at the seaside. He jumped into his boat and instantly started to accelerate. He needed to get out to sea as fast as possible.

Within minutes, he saw the first wave. Sugawara craned his neck as *Sunflower* charged the wall of water. It looked as if it was at least 60 feet high.

"You've been with me 42 years, *Sunflower*," Sugawara whispered, his voice catching in his throat. "If we live or die, then we'll be together." The quiet sea captain gunned the throttle and drove directly into the wave. The boat climbed so high it made him dizzy. Knowing he was no longer in control, Sugawara closed his eyes. When he opened them, he realized he had crested the wave. *Sunflower* was on a gentle descent on the other side of it.

Together, Sugawara and *Sunflower* crossed wave after wave. Some of the giant beasts came close to tugging the old boat under their crushing force, but somehow *Sunflower* brought Sugawara to safety. After the last wave, Sugawara saw the horizon. The sea was completely calm. It was as if the nightmare had never happened.

Katsunobu Sakurai

City Hall, Minamisoma, Japan,
March 11, 2011, 3:27 p.m.

When the tremors of the quake stopped, nearly everyone in the old Minamisoma city hall building fled to the parking lot. They didn't want to be indoors in case of a collapse.

People clustered in pairs and small groups, bracing themselves against the chilly wind. Many tried calling and texting loved ones, but they couldn't get through. The cell network was surely overloaded by the high volume of people trying to reach one another after the disaster.

Mayor Sakurai watched all of this but didn't join the group outside. Instead, he and a few colleagues jogged up the stairs of the building and stepped out onto the flat roof. From this vantage point, they could survey the damage the earthquake had caused. Homes with collapsed roofs and overturned cars dotted the landscape.

When Sakurai looked to the horizon, he saw a giant cloud of dust rising into the air. "Is that a fire?" he asked.

"No," his colleague replied. "That is the tsunami hitting the shoreline."

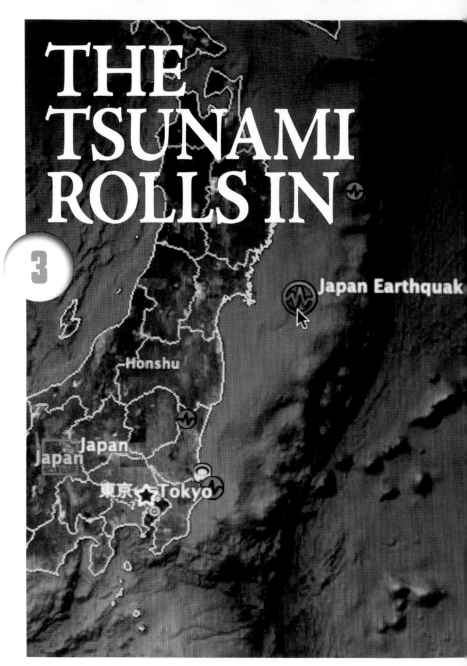

THE TSUNAMI ROLLS IN

3

Japan Earthquak

Honshu

Japan

Japan

東京 ☆ Tokyo

With a magnitude of 9.0, the March 2011 earthquake was the most powerful to hit Japan and the fourth-largest earthquake worldwide since 1900.

Atsufumi Yoshizawa

Control Room, Fukushima Dai-Ichi, March 11, 2011, 3:30 p.m.

Yoshizawa sat on the corner of a desk in the brightly lit control room and busily scratched notes into his journal. Information about the state of the plant was pouring in, and he needed to keep everything straight. All around him, managers of Fukushima Dai-Ichi were busy working to bring the giant nuclear power plant back to its feet.

Several employees were seriously injured and others were missing. Some parts of the plant had sustained serious damage in the quake. Thankfully, the nuclear reactors had survived. Yoshizawa breathed easier knowing that at least there was no threat of a nuclear meltdown.

Suddenly, a worker burst into the room. "A tsunami has hit the plant!" he cried. "It's a giant tsunami!"

Astufumi instinctively looked toward the walls of the room, but of course, there were no windows. The control room was heavily fortified with thick concrete walls. It was built to sustain a natural disaster. He and the other managers had no idea what was happening outside.

A minute later, another worker ran through the open door of the control room. "The seawall has been breached. Water is rushing into the plant!" he shouted.

Yoshizawa looked at the plant's manager, Masao Yoshida. He looked stunned. Just then, another messenger walked into the room looking ashen. The room fell silent as everyone waited to hear the latest news.

"Cars are floating past the plant," the messenger said quietly. *"And an oil tanker . . . I saw . . . I saw an oil tanker float by the plant . . . this is unbelievable."*

As Yoshizawa struggled to wrap his mind around this latest detail, the control room received more bad news. The backup generators in reactors 1 to 5 had flooded and stopped working. This meant that the systems designed to keep the nuclear reactors from overheating had failed. As if overheating reactors weren't terrifying enough, another shocking update followed: the system's seawater pumps, designed to siphon off some of the heat created by each reactor, had also failed. The combined loss of the seawater pumps and the cooling systems meant that the reactors were heating up, and fast. This meant that a disaster could be imminent.

Yoshizawa knew the situation had suddenly become very, very dangerous.

Leticia Morales

USS Ronald Reagan,
March 11, 2011

Master Chief Petty Officer Leticia Morales had a few minutes before her next personnel meeting, so she decided to head up to the deck of the USS

Ronald Reagan to get a bit of sunshine. The *Reagan* was a 77,000-ton aircraft carrier en route to Busan, South Korea.

As she stepped out onto the deck, she gazed out at the beautiful blue ocean. She had been in the Navy since she was 19, and had worked on board the *Ronald Reagan* for three years. She loved the Navy and the structure it gave her life. She also loved being able to travel the world and help people in need.

Just then, she heard the crackle of the ship's public address system. "This is Captain Burke," the familiar voice began. "I have an announcement."

Morales was surprised when Burke went on to tell the crew about a terrible earthquake and tsunami that had struck the northeastern part of Japan. The ship was changing course. It was heading to Japan on a humanitarian mission to provide aid.

Good, Morales thought to herself. *This is what we do. We help people.* She hoped the ship could make good time. She and her shipmates had provided aid after a 2008 typhoon struck the Philippines, and she knew how crucial it was to get to the victims as quickly as possible.

Some of Morales' shipmates went online to research the situation in Japan as they sailed toward the disaster site. They learned that thousands of people were feared missing or dead. They also discovered that while most of Japan's nuclear reactors in the area had safely shut down, one was experiencing trouble. The government had even evacuated thousands of people who lived within 2 miles of the plant. While this information seemed troubling, the Japanese government was very reassuring. They announced that no radioactive materials had been detected in the area.

Destructive tsunami waves traveled up to 6 miles inland in Sendai, just north of Fukushima.

Takashi Sato

Takashi Sato nervously paced around the control room. The earthquake hadn't scared him, but the loss of backup power in the plant had left him feeling absolutely terrified.

The young plant inspector couldn't believe what had happened. Before today, he had thought of the plant as the place he would flee to in case of an emergency.

Now, Sato realized, the plant wasn't a safe haven. In fact, it was a ticking time bomb.

Sato joined a crew of electricians, engineers, and other plant workers who had assembled in the control room. The rest of the plant was still in the dark. The electronic monitors that provided essential readings on the temperature and energy levels in each reactor were black. The phones weren't working. A few laptops were operational, but their batteries were slowly draining. The workers needed to find a way to power their instruments so that they could monitor the status of the nuclear reactors. And they needed to do it quickly.

A worker wondered out loud if it might be possible to find enough car batteries to power the circuit boards that provided readings on the reactors. It sounded crazy, but it also sounded like it might work. A group of workers jogged out to the parking lot and came back with a dozen car batteries. They wired them to the control panel monitoring reactor 1. Soon, the flickering lights of the instrument panel told them they had succeeded. As power flooded back into the monitors, the workers learned that the nuclear reactor's heat and pressure had built to dangerous levels.

One engineer asked, "Are we in trouble? Isn't this dangerous?"

His questions were met with silence.

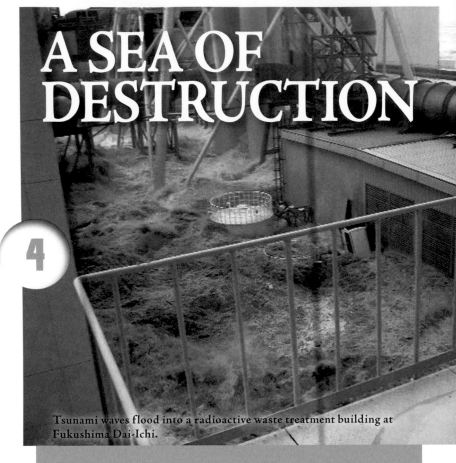

A SEA OF DESTRUCTION

4

Tsunami waves flood into a radioactive waste treatment building at Fukushima Dai-Ichi.

Naoto Kan

Prime Minister's Office,
Tokyo, Japan, March 12, 2011, 5:44 a.m.

Prime Minister Naoto Kan nodded to his aide. He was issuing yet another official government order: the evacuation zone around

the Fukushima Dai-Ichi nuclear plant was expanding. It now included anyone within 6 miles of the disaster. *How on earth has this happened?* he thought to himself for what felt like the thousandth time since it happened.

The gruff, tough-talking politician had been up all night. He and a close group of his trusted advisors were monitoring his country's response to the epic earthquake and tsunami. And now, he was struggling to stay on top of a potential nuclear catastrophe.

Kan was tired and frustrated. He wasn't getting enough information from TEPCO about the status of the reactors. He was worried that the plant was unstable. From the small amount of information TEPCO had released, he and his advisors had pieced together enough to understand that the situation was dire.

The prime minister was used to butting heads with businesses and bureaucrats. Back in the 1990s, he had worked as Japan's health minister. When he discovered that the ministry had been knowingly administering blood tainted with HIV to sick patients, he was outraged. He exposed the scandal to the public. He immediately earned a reputation for being a rabble-rouser. Unlike so many others in the Japanese government, Kan wasn't afraid to stand up to the establishment and fight for what he thought was right.

A TEPCO spokesperson told Kan and his advisors that the plant's backup generators had lost power. This meant that there wasn't any water keeping the reactors cool. The water around the reactors was getting so hot that it was boiling. This was creating enormous amounts of steam and pressure inside the reactor buildings. TEPCO scientists were worried that the reactors might explode. They asked Kan and his team for permission to open vents in the reactor buildings to let some of the steam out and reduce the pressure.

Naoto Kan (third from right) leads a meeting of government officials in Tokyo on March 12, 2011.

Just one day earlier, a request like this would have seemed preposterous. The steam contained harmful radiation. Releasing it into the environment would spread the radiation and possibly harm living things nearby. However, Kan and his team knew that if a small amount of radioactive steam wasn't released, the entire reactor could explode, releasing huge quantities of radiation that could kill living things within hundreds of miles. Kan gave the approval to TEPCO to start venting the reactors.

The prime minister and his team waited anxiously for news from the plant. Minutes ticked by. After nearly an hour, the venting still hadn't occurred. Knowing that each moment that passed increased the risk of a nuclear explosion, Kan decided to mobilize. He and his team boarded a Self-Defense Forces helicopter and took off for the plant. The prime minister knew he could be an intimidating presence. Maybe, he thought, a little face-to-face time would be enough to scare the management into action.

As his helicopter soared north, away from the booming metropolis of Tokyo and along the northeastern coast of Japan, Kan leaned forward in his plush seat to look out the chopper's clean, bulletproof window. Suddenly, all of his irritation with TEPCO vanished. He was overcome with horror and sadness. One after another, he watched as ravaged coastal villages appeared below his window. Homes were splintered. Buildings had crumbled. Gigantic boats lay on their sides in the middle of neighborhoods. Despite the water that seemed to be everywhere he looked, fires raged wildly. He wondered how many poor souls had died, and how many would never be found.

When his chopper touched down at Fukushima Dai-Ichi at 7:00 a.m., Kan was sad, overwhelmed, and angry.

Masao Yoshida

Control Room, Fukushima Dai-Ichi,
March 12, 2011, 7:30 a.m.

The last person Masao Yoshida expected to see at his workplace was the prime minister of Japan. But sure enough, Naoto Kan had just marched into the plant's control room.

"What is going on?" Kan barked at Yoshida. "Why haven't you started venting yet?"

Yoshida took a deep breath. The answer was complicated, but it was important for the prime minister to understand that they were doing everything they could to obey his orders.

"Normally, we would use electric power to open the vents. We don't have power, so we are trying to open them by hand," he said.

One of his colleagues interrupted. "But prime minister, the radiation levels near the vents are very high. It is very dangerous inside there. Allowing workers near the vents means they could be killed from radiation exposure."

Yoshida cut his colleague off. "We will do the venting," he said sternly. "We will do it even if we have to form a suicide corps."

Kan seemed to understand this. He nodded at Yoshida.

Yoshida and a group of workers gathered together to decide how to tackle the problem. They knew that the radiation levels were so high that they could only spend a very short amount of time near the vents before they were killed by the radiation. They decided to take the job in shifts. Dressed in thick protective gear and breathing oxygen from a tank, pairs of workers would hurry in, do as much work as they could, then hurry out. Another set would replace them and continue the work.

Working quickly and efficiently, Yoshida's team successfully opened the vent for reactor 1 just enough to release the rapidly building pressure. They hesitantly celebrated the results of their hard work. At that moment it seemed as though things were finally starting to come under control.

Naoto Kan

Prime Minister's Office,
Tokyo, Japan, March 12, 2011, 3:36 p.m.

"Prime minister, the nuclear plant is exploding! The TV is showing it now!"

Manabu Terada, the prime minister's special advisor, had just burst into Kan's office. He was out of breath and clearly panicked. An aide hurried to turn on the television and find the news. When the images flickered onto the screen, Kan's jaw dropped. He couldn't believe it. He had just been there this morning.

Kan watched as a slow-motion replay showed smoke mushrooming out of one of the plant's buildings. He wondered what he was seeing; whether it was an explosion of water vapor, or a more lethal release of toxic radiation. Instantly, he started thinking about Chernobyl, the Ukrainian nuclear plant that had suffered a catastrophic meltdown in 1986. That disaster had killed dozens, injured hundreds, and made an entire city unlivable.

Sitting near Kan was Haruki Madarame, the nuclear safety commission chief.

Kan turned to the chief and angrily asked, "What's going on?"

Others in the room joined in. "Is this a Chernobyl-type explosion?" they asked.

"Is this the same thing that happened at Chernobyl?"

Their questions were frantic and panicked. Madarame sat in silence, watching the footage with his head in his hands. He didn't speak. Or perhaps he couldn't.

The news reporter announced that a hydrogen explosion had occurred inside reactor 1. The force of the blast blew the roof off the reactor building and collapsed the walls surrounding the pool where the used nuclear fuel was stored. This meant that the nuclear substances inside were now releasing toxic radiation directly into the air around the reactor.

FINDING SOLUTIONS

5

Explosions caused crippling damage to important structures at
Fukushima Dai-Ichi.

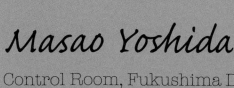

   Masao Yoshida knew that if he
wasn't able to cool the reactors down,
the world was in grave danger. Venting,
Yoshida knew, was only buying time.
It wasn't a solution to the rapidly
escalating problem.

   Yoshida needed to find a way to
lower the temperatures inside the
reactors. Since his generators and
cooling systems were out of commission,
he had to think creatively. The plant
was located right on the sea. Maybe, he
thought, he could pump seawater into
the reactors. He knew the corrosive
saltwater could ruin the reactors for
future use, but he wasn't worried about
that. His thoughts were focused only on
preventing a meltdown. He proposed the

idea to the TEPCO management, who told him to wait while they ran the plan by the prime minister.

At 7:04 p.m., Yoshida decided it was too dangerous to continue waiting. He ordered his team to start pumping seawater into reactor 1.

Minutes after he began, Yoshida's phone rang. It was TEPCO's Ichiro Takekuro. "Halt the seawater injection," he ordered. "We are still discussing it in the prime minister's office now."

Yoshida could hardly believe his ears. He assembled his team around him and called the TEPCO headquarters in Tokyo to get their take on the situation. They echoed Takekuro's sentiment: "We have to halt the injection because we do not have the blessing from Prime Minister Kan."

Inside the Fukushima Dai-Ichi control room, the tired workers exchanged confused looks. Yoshida felt sure they were all wondering the same thing. Why would they stop the seawater injection? It was the only thing standing between them and a nuclear meltdown.

Yoshida placed his hand over the speaker on the phone and whispered to his team: "By all means, never stop the water injection." Then, in a loud voice, he announced to the phone, "Stop the seawater injection!"

His team understood. They continued the seawater injection. When TEPCO and the prime minister finally agreed to start injecting seawater, Yoshida's team had already been doing it for more than an hour.

Leticia Morales

USS *Ronald Reagan*,
Just off the Japanese coast, March 12, 2011

Leticia Morales was belowdeck when it happened. The USS *Ronald Reagan* was charging toward northeastern Japan to provide aid to those injured in the earthquake and tsunami. The mission was being called Operation Tomodachi, which meant Operation Friends.

As the giant aircraft carrier barreled through the water, many of Morales' shipmates on deck were experiencing a mild snowstorm. The fluffy flakes softly floated down toward the speeding ship.

Abruptly, the ship glided into a warm pocket of air. The snowflakes vanished. A harsh, metallic taste filled Morales' mouth. Her tongue suddenly felt like it was coated in metal. She smacked her lips a few times and took a drink from her bottle of water. As soon as the taste had appeared, it was gone. She didn't think much of it and continued her work.

USS *Ronald Reagan*, March 2011

Prime Minister Kan opened the folder he had just been handed. It was another progress report giving him an update on the state of his country.

Expert witnesses on the ground were estimating that more than 100,000 private homes were damaged or lost due to the tsunami waves, which had struck from Hokaido all the way to Okinawa. Sendai, a city of over one million people, had been hit hard by the tsunami. Not only were many of the city's roads and homes damaged, its airport had been destroyed.

As Kan continued reading the report, the details became more and more unbelievable. An entire passenger train seemed to have gone missing. The coastal city of Kesennuma was burning, with no way for locals to fight the raging fires. A petrochemical complex in the Miyagi Prefecture had suffered a giant explosion.

News from the Fukushima Dai-Ichi plant wasn't any better. TEPCO officials had taken new readings from the area around the plant and found that radiation was leaking into the atmosphere. Water levels inside reactor 2 were falling, which meant that the nuclear fuel inside was heating up. Kan and his team agreed to issue a new order of evacuation for residents living within 12 miles of the plant.

The people of northeastern Japan were in trouble. Their communities had been ravaged. Many, he knew, were ignoring evacuation orders to search for missing loved ones. Kan needed help bringing his country back to order. The United States had rushed to his aid, promising the help of its aircraft carrier, the USS *Ronald Reagan*. Kan hoped it would arrive soon.

Morales could hardly believe her eyes. The ship had arrived off the coast of northeastern Japan earlier in the day. The gleaming aircraft carrier had become an island in a sea of destruction. Everywhere she looked, she saw wreckage from the disaster. The surface of the water appeared solid with metal, plastic, and wood. She watched as a roof from a house floated out into the sea. One of her shipmates called out from the other side of the deck that he could see a car bobbing in the water. Morales couldn't help but wonder how many bodies were floating under the debris.

Morales and the rest of the crew busily prepared to disembark and get their aid mission underway. Shortly after they had arrived, Captain Burke made an announcement over the ship's PA system that a nearby nuclear plant had suffered an explosion.

He assured his crew that they had nothing to worry about.

Morales trusted the captain's judgment, even after receiving several worried emails from her family. Her father had worked in a nuclear power facility in the United States and was very concerned about the Fukushima Dai-Ichi plant. He warned her to drink only bottled water and take potassium iodine tablets. He told her that these tablets could stop radiation from being absorbed by the thyroid gland. Morales just chuckled as she read his emails. She felt sure that her thyroid would be just fine. Despite his warnings to stay away from the plant and the irradiated surroundings, Morales volunteered to go into the mainland by helicopter so that she could provide hands-on assistance to the victims.

Tsunami waves tossed around huge objects
such as ships, adding them to the widespread
masses of coastal debris.

MELTDOWN

The inside of reactor 3 at Fukushima Dai-Ichi, before the building
experienced a hydrogen explosion

Masao Yoshida

Control Room, Fukushima Dai-Ichi,
March 14, 2011, 11:01 a.m.

This has to be a nightmare, Masao
Yoshida thought. *Surely, I will wake up soon.*

Yoshida gripped the edge of a desk and
closed his eyes. A deafening blast had just
ripped through the plant. Yoshida knew
exactly what the noise had been — it was a
hydrogen explosion in reactor 3.

Instantly, the control room erupted
into a frenzy of work as plant workers
once again tried to assess the state of the
rapidly deteriorating nuclear plant. This
sense of panic and disaster was becoming
terribly familiar.

Yoshida and his team had done
everything they could to avoid this latest
explosion. They had been pumping seawater
into the hot reactor and venting air for more

than a day. Their efforts, it seemed, had been in vain.

Reports quickly poured into the control room that the blast in reactor 3 had been powerful. It had damaged the structure of the building surrounding the reactor and exposed a pool of used radioactive fuel to the open air. This was exactly what Yoshida had feared. The nuclear reactors at Fukushima Dai-Ichi had been constructed carefully, with many layers of protection keeping the nuclear fuel sealed inside. However, these buildings could only withstand so much damage.

Reactor 3 was just one of Yoshida's problems. The water levels in reactors 1 and 2 were also falling. This meant that the dangerous nuclear fuel inside was being exposed to the air inside the sealed reactor buildings. If the structure of either of these buildings was damaged, radioactive substances could easily leak out into the surroundings. That would be a critically dangerous situation.

The day before, Yukio Edano, the chief cabinet secretary, had made an announcement to the public that a partial meltdown at the Fukushima Dai-Ichi plant was "highly possible."

In a true nuclear meltdown, extremely hot nuclear fuel could actually melt the structure of a reactor. Eventually the reactor's structure might be damaged so much that enormous amounts of dangerous radiation could leak out into the surroundings and be hazardous to living things.

As Yoshida mentally reviewed the status of reactors 1, 2, and 3, he agreed with the chief cabinet secretary's statement. It was looking more and more possible that the plant would suffer a meltdown.

Takashi Sato

Control Room, Fukushima Dai-Ichi, March 14, 2011, 11:05 a.m.

"We're finished," a colleague muttered.

Plant inspector Takashi Sato hated to admit it, but he agreed. The sound of the last explosion was terrifying. The blast had broken windows around the plant, and the noise of shattering glass had felt deafening.

I will never leave this plant. I will die here, Sato thought as he scanned the room full of panicked workers. He overheard two men urgently whispering to one another. Sato stepped closer to hear what they were saying.

"We could flee," one said quietly, staring at his shoes. The other nodded silently.

What weaklings, Sato thought. But still, he had to acknowledge that he had considered leaving as well.

Updates from outside the plant were far from reassuring. The Japanese government was frantically working to get the country running smoothly again after a disaster of epic proportions. Sato had heard a group of supervisors muttering that 50,000 Japan Self-Defense Forces personnel had deployed to the area to aid victims. He also heard something about many aircraft carriers being sent their way. Sato wondered bleakly if there was any way for them to help the workers stuck inside the nuclear plant.

Masao Yoshida

"I have something to discuss," Yoshida announced. "Please, everyone. Gather around."

The control room was full of weary employees. They had been working around the clock trying to prevent a full nuclear meltdown for nearly five days. Piles of coats and sweaters dotted the corners of the room. Workers had been using them as pillows and blankets as they napped in shifts in the loud, brightly lit room. The team was hungry. They had been living on rations of dried biscuits and were restricted to one half-liter bottle of water every two days.

They badly needed supplies, such as food, water, and protective suits for workers to wear near the reactors. But they knew that they were not the only people struggling in Japan at the moment. People all around the northeast were still being pulled from the wreckage of the tsunami and earthquake. The workers' needs, it seemed, would have to wait.

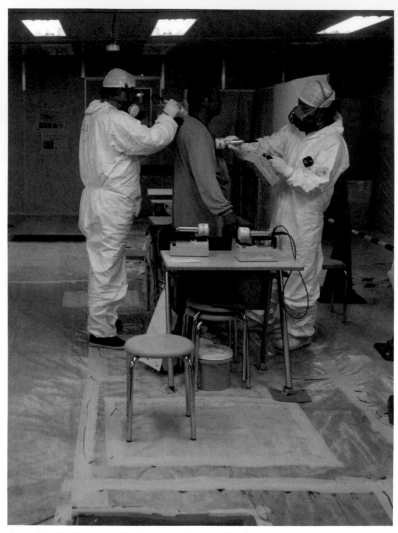

A worker is given a radiation screening inside the
crippled Fukushima Dai-Ichi plant.

The day before had brought new disasters. A hydrogen explosion had ripped through the reactor 2 building, and a fire had erupted inside the reactor 4 building. Deadly radiation smoke had snaked out into the sky, spreading fear inside its black plumes.

Radiation measurements around the plant confirmed everyone's fears. The deadly substance was, indeed, leaking. And the levels were frighteningly high. Yoshida knew the numbers by heart: on average, people typically absorb about 3 millisieverts of radiation a year. This radiation comes from all sorts of sources, ranging from X-rays to microwaves. In these low levels, radiation is harmless. Nuclear plant workers are typically restricted to absorbing 20–50 millisieverts of radiation per year. This was a higher dose than the average person's exposure, but still considered very safe. But the latest readings around the plant showed unbelievable results: the plant was emitting radiation at a rate of 400 millisieverts per *hour*. At this rate, Yoshida knew, any type of prolonged exposure could be deadly.

"Can everyone hear me?" Yoshida coughed. His voice was hoarse from exhaustion. He sipped from one of the scarce water bottles inside the control room.

"You have all worked bravely," he told the group of more than 200 workers.

"You have pumped seawater into the reactors. You have vented the reactors. You have nursed your fellow workers' injuries. You have risked your lives."

Some of the workers nodded, gravely. Others looked down at their shoes.

"As most of you know, the government has expanded the evacuation zone to anyone within 19 miles of this area. Radiation has escaped the plant in high levels. We know that several of the reactors are damaged, and we suspect that further damage will occur as the temperatures of the fuel continue to rise."

Yoshida sighed and glanced down at his notes.

"Emperor Akihito has even made a special appearance on television. He has reminded us all to understand and help one another. And now, I feel as though I must help you. Starting now, we are going to evacuate. Just go home. We've done this much. We can do no more. Just go home."

Takashi Sato

Takashi Sato was flooded with relief as he listened to Manager Yoshida tell everyone to go home. He did not want to be a coward, but he wanted to leave the plant as soon as possible. His thoughts were always of his wife and daughter. Several times over the last few days, he was sure he was going to die. He found himself mentally scanning his body, wondering if he had absorbed too much radiation.

He packed up his briefcase and, along with many other weary workers, made his way outside. He was finally going home.

A large group of workers had chosen to remain behind at the plant to continue their work. Sato was grateful for their bravery, but he was also thrilled at the chance to leave.

Atsufumi Yoshizawa stepped outside of the crisis center. He was only 3 miles away from the Fukushima Dai-Ichi nuclear plant, but if he looked to the bright blue sky, he could imagine that he was on the other side of the world. For a brief moment, he listened to the birds chirp and felt the brisk breeze on his cheeks.

When he dropped his gaze to the parking lot, he realized that he had an audience. A group of firefighters, police, soldiers, and nuclear officials had gathered to watch as he and his colleagues left the safe house. They had enjoyed a three-day break from the constant terror and panic of the plant. But now, they were heading back to do their best. They had given up hope of saving the plant. Now they were simply hoping to prevent further disaster.

He looked at the crowd. Their expressions were bleak. One by one, they lifted their hands and saluted. Yoshizawa understood their message. They believed that he and his colleagues were like the Tokkotai, the kamikaze pilots of World War II. They were going to sacrifice themselves in order to fulfill their duty.

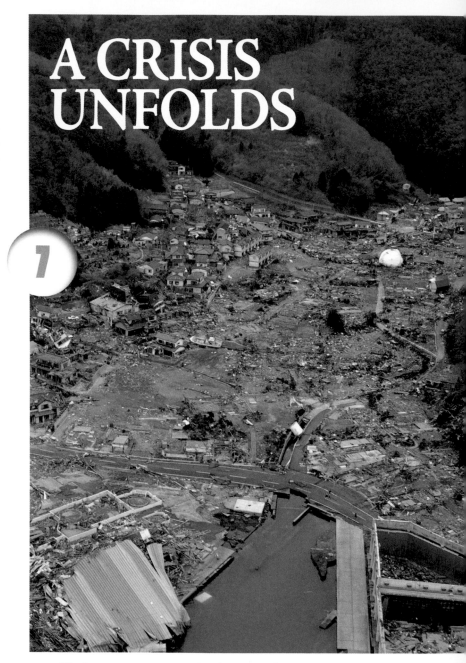

A CRISIS
UNFOLDS

7

The Japanese government faced a massive humanitarian crisis in tsunami-ravaged areas, even as a nuclear catastrophe unfolded at Fukushima Dai-Ichi.

Naoto Kan

Prime Minister Naoto Kan gazed at his desk, covered with folders from different agencies, each containing updates on the crisis. He had just reviewed the latest progress report from the Fukushima Dai-Ichi plant, and things were just as grim as ever.

The latest attempt to cool the reactors had failed. Kan had watched the mission on live TV along with millions of other Japanese. Military helicopters had flown over the plant and dumped water into the superheated reactors. It had been a risky operation. The pilots were flying in high winds near an unstable nuclear plant. And now it seemed that all of the danger they had faced was for nothing. The fuel inside the reactors continued to rage.

Radiation had leaked from the plant. Kan knew this much for sure. Just that morning, he had been informed that tap water and milk in the Fukushima area contained radioactive materials. He just hoped that it wouldn't spread beyond the immediate area around the plant.

Just then, his smartphone pinged. One of his advisors had messaged him. He opened the text and felt his heart drop into his stomach.

"Test results in. Tokyo tap water contains elevated levels of radiation."

Tokyo was about 140 miles away from the plant. Kan tried to remain calm as he wondered how far this disaster would reach.

Atsufumi Yoshizawa

Control Room, Fukushima Dai-Ichi,
March 21, 2011

Atsufumi Yoshizawa sat on the floor of the control room to eat his lunch of instant noodles. He thought about the good news that he'd just heard.

The temperatures inside reactors 5 and 6 were starting to stabilize. This meant that those reactors were not in danger of melting down. Power had been restored to reactors 1, 2, 5, and 6.

For the first time in 10 days, it seemed like he might actually make it out of the plant alive.

Yoshizawa looked at the whiteboard on the other side of the room. On it was a list of names. Each of the workers who stayed at the plant after the evacuation had written his name on it. Plant manager Yoshida had insisted on it. In his darker moments, Yoshizawa had wondered if it was going to become their final memorial.

He slurped down the last bite of his noodles and smiled at a colleague. For the first time in days, he

A Japanese police officer searches for missing people within the evacuation zone near Fukushima Dai-Ichi.

dared to feel hopeful. "We are going to make it out of here!" he exclaimed.

His colleague just grimaced.

"What's bothering you?" Yoshizawa asked. "Today is a good day!"

"We will have cancer after 10 years, won't we?" his colleague asked.

Yoshizawa fell silent. He didn't have an answer.

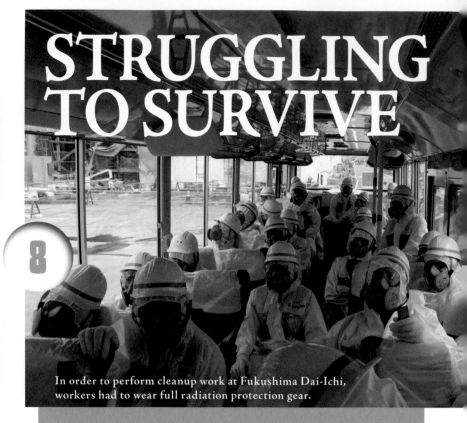

In order to perform cleanup work at Fukushima Dai-Ichi, workers had to wear full radiation protection gear.

Naoto Kan

Tokyo, Japan,
March 25, 2011

Prime Minister Naoto Kan stepped onto the small stage and walked to the podium. In front of him were rows of folding chairs filled with reporters and photographers. Instead of his usual crisp black

business suit, he wore a blue work suit. It was meant to show his solidarity with the workers toiling in the rapidly decaying nuclear plant.

"My fellow citizens," he began, "the situation at the Fukushima Nuclear Plant remains grave and serious."

Kan took a deep breath. He knew this was not the news the press was hoping to hear. His administration had been promising progress and hard work for the last two weeks. But though they had done everything in their power to contain the radiation leaking from the plant, they simply could not guarantee the safety of those living near it.

They had recently expanded the voluntary evacuation zone to include those within 18 miles of the plant. He worried that any escalation in the crisis at the plant might lead to police forcing people out of their homes. That was the last thing the people of Japan needed.

"Radiation, we now know, has leaked from the plant. It has been found in the water and soil. And now, scientists have found traces of radioactivity in 11 types of vegetables that were grown in the Fukushima area. We have also detected radioactivity in milk from dairy farms near the plant. The government is imposing an immediate ban on the export or sale of these products until we can guarantee that they are safe for consumption."

Kan lifted his gaze to the crowd. Cameras clicked and shuttered. Journalists scribbled in their notepads. He knew this news would be met with panic. This was exactly what the public had feared. But he had to be honest. He had to confront the danger and do his best to stop it. Just as he had with the Health Ministry crisis in the 1990s, he was willing to admit problems in order to solve them.

"We are not in a position where we can be optimistic. We must treat every development with the utmost care," he continued.

Kan hoped he was done delivering bad news, but he had a feeling he was just getting started.

Masao Yoshida

"Call 119! Someone, call 119!" Plant Manager Masao Yoshida shouted into the busy control room. An ambulance was needed immediately. He hoped the emergency phone line was working.

Yoshida had approved the mission himself. He had sent three workers to replace electrical cables in the flooded basement of the building of reactor 3. As they waded through the highly irradiated water, two of the workers felt the toxic liquid seep through their protective boots and soak their skin. They immediately fled the scene as their skin painfully bubbled and burned from the exposure. The third worker helped carry the injured men out of the basement, then sprinted to find help.

While Yoshida waited for the ambulance to arrive, he nervously paced the room. The moans of the injured men filled his ears.

He was consumed with guilt. His employees were trying to work in a minefield of radiation. It wasn't just dangerous inside the plant. The surroundings were showing frightening levels of radiation as well. Just two days earlier, TEPCO had found that the radioactive iodine levels in the wastewater just south of the plant were nearly 130 times the legal limit. Tokyo's tap water continued to show traces of radioactive materials.

The small victories his team had achieved seemed insignificant in the face of such danger. They had managed to restore power to all the plant's control rooms. They had also continued to inject seawater into the superheated reactors, trying their best to keep them cool.

Finally the emergency crews had arrived. The injured men were helped out of the building and into an ambulance. Yoshida noticed that the ambulance workers were dressed in white protective suits that covered their entire bodies. He realized that even coming into contact with the injured workers presented a radiation threat to the paramedics.

How will we ever survive this? he wondered. Then, accepting that he might die at this nuclear plant, he returned to work.

Workers in radiation suits perform tasks to restore the power grid at Fukushima Dai-Ichi.

PLEADING FOR HELP

9

The Japanese government estimated that the earthquake and tsunami caused $300 billion in total damages.

Katsunobu Sakurai

City Hall, Minamisoma, Japan,
March 24, 2011

Mayor Sakurai looked straight into the lens of the digital video camera. The last two weeks had aged him considerably. He knew he looked tired, gaunt, and desperate.

Minamisoma was in grave danger. It had not only suffered from the earthquake and tsunami, but it was now cut off from the rest of the world by the threat of nuclear radiation seeping from the nearby Fukushima Dai-Ichi plant. The 20,000 residents who hadn't immediately vacated their homes were now trapped inside, warned repeatedly by officials that any time spent outside could expose them to dangerous levels of radiation.

These townspeople were now running low on food, water, and fuel. Many were injured. Some were even starving. And Mayor Sakurai had no idea when their plight would end. He wasn't getting answers to his questions from the government or TEPCO. He wanted to know when the threat would lift, how his city would be helped, and what resources were available to him. So far, it seemed he was being overlooked.

Resting his hands on the folding table in front of him, he began the hardest speech he had ever given: "I would like to thank all of those who have offered to help. But . . . we are left isolated."

"We ask for your help, volunteers. We need help to transport supplies, but we must depend on volunteers who could act at their own risk because of the measures to remain indoors issued by the government. . . . We urge the media to come here and witness what is developing here. Since the measure to remain indoors has been taken, all the stores and supermarkets are shut down, the banks are closed, the people are literally drying up as if they are under starvation tactics."

Mayor Sakurai took a deep breath. This humbling plea for help was very difficult for him. But his people were in trouble, and he could think of no other way to save them.

"Local officials are now fighting the threat of radiation," he continued. "They have been working to protect the citizens in such a strain and exhaustion. Some of them lost their family in the earthquake disaster, and some lost their houses. They are the backbones of the lives of the citizens."

Mayor Sakurai shifted uncomfortably. A clock chimed. He finished his message with a final plea to his audience:

"I beg you, as the mayor of Minamisoma city, to help us. Helping each other is what makes us human beings."

He nodded to his assistant to turn off the camera. Gone were the days of bustling press conferences filled with eager journalists. Now, his only means of communicating with the world was through the Internet. His assistant uploaded the video onto YouTube, and the two sat back and stared at the computer screen. The only thing they could do was hope.

Employee X

It had been just over two weeks since the earthquake had changed everything. Employee X had been working grueling hours as he tried to help bring the plant back under control.

A few days earlier, he had received an email from an acquaintance working at TEPCO's headquarters in Tokyo. He probably should have ignored it, maybe even deleted it. But he couldn't bring himself to do so. Instead, he secretly began emailing with him.

In his response, Employee X had written, "Though we're still in the middle of our fight, we feel a little relieved to know we have the support from people like you. But also, I just want people to understand that there are many people fighting under harsh circumstances in the nuclear plants. Crying is useless," he continued. "If we're in hell now, all we can do is crawl up towards heaven."

Employee X's TEPCO friend responded quickly: "I feel frustrating anger across the nation pointing to TEPCO. I suspect TEPCO executives feel it well enough."

Employee X had to agree. "The quake," he wrote, "is a natural disaster. But TEPCO should be blamed for contamination caused by the radioactive materials released from the nuclear plants. . . . I'm not saying workers at nuclear plants are bad! I'm not saying anyone is bad! But most workers in the plants are local residents. All of us, including myself, are victims of the disaster. The scene here is completely like a war zone . . . but we will fight until the end."

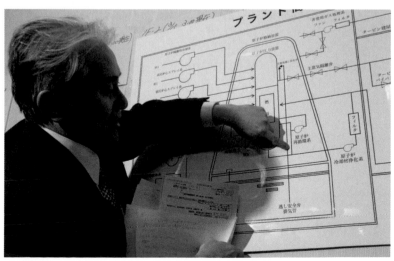

Speaking at a press conference, a TEPCO official answers reporters' questions about the Fukushima disaster.

AFTERMATH

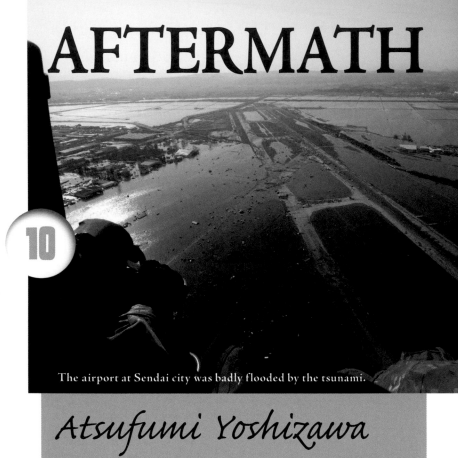

The airport at Sendai city was badly flooded by the tsunami.

Atsufumi Yoshizawa

Toyko, Japan,
April 8, 2011

Atsufumi Yoshizawa stepped out of the train station and into the brisk spring air. The streets of Tokyo were bustling. Businesspeople rushed to meetings. Mothers pushed babies in strollers.

Taxicabs and buses zoomed by. Life in Tokyo seemed completely normal.

Yoshizawa sat down on a bench to rest and noticed that no one sat next to him. He couldn't blame people for keeping their distance. After all, he knew he looked terrible. He hadn't shaved or showered in four weeks. He was wearing a tracksuit that no longer fit him; it was far too big for his now-thin frame.

He wondered what his family would think when they saw him. He was so eager to be with them, even if it was only for three days. This break from the constant pressure at the plant would be good for him. He knew he would return to work recharged and rested. And he couldn't wait to eat something other than instant noodles.

As he waited for his ride home, Yoshizawa's thoughts turned to his colleagues. Some of them were on similar weekend breaks. He hoped their families were OK. He knew many of them were heading home to attend funerals. Yoshizawa and his colleagues had bonded in a way that he never could have expected. He felt like they had fought in a war together. As though they were soldiers on the front lines. Except, he thought, their enemy was not an army. It was a nuclear plant.

Yoshizawa knew that the country had turned against TEPCO. He had watched the reports from inside the radiation-proof bunker at the plant. People suspected that the nuclear disaster had been avoidable, that the workers at Fukushima had made mistakes. It was difficult to hear. Especially as he and his colleagues worked as hard as they could to protect the people of Japan from a nuclear plant that was spinning out of control. But at the same time he understood their anger.

"I will take responsibility," he muttered to himself. "But I will also work hard to ensure that this never happens again. Never."

Naoto Kan

There had been hundreds of aftershocks since the quake. Most of them were minor — strong enough to stop people in their tracks, but not enough to really scare anyone. Prime Minister Kan had yet to duck under his desk during any of them. But yesterday's was different. He had been scheduled to give a speech on the one-month anniversary of the tsunami, earthquake, and nuclear disaster, but a magnitude 6.4 aftershock changed his plans. It had triggered a landslide, destroyed homes, and killed at least six people. *This*, Kan thought, sighing, *on top of everything else the Japanese people have been through.*

His team had worked efficiently, rescheduling his speech for today while also managing the ongoing disaster relief operations around the country.

As he stepped to the podium to speak, he reminded the journalists present to stay calm in the case of another aftershock.

He was holding this press conference for many reasons. He wanted to mark the anniversary of the tragedy that had struck Japan, but he also needed to

Naoto Kan visited a devastated city in Japan's Iwate Prefecture, April 2011.

show that he was in control. Too many skeptics had accused his administration of not doing a good job of handling the enormous effort of bringing Japan back onto its feet.

He also needed to share some bad news. For weeks, the nuclear disaster had been classified as a Level 5 event on the International Nuclear Events Scale. This was on a scale of 1 to 7, so while it was clearly serious, it was not the worst possible type of disaster. Despite this ranking, it seemed clear that the public had grown deeply suspicious that the government was not telling them how dangerous the situation really was. Today, Kan was going to break the news that their suspicions were correct.

He started his speech by thanking those who had helped Japan in this crisis, and by expressing his condolences for those who lost loved ones in the disaster. He then took a deep breath and looked down at his notes. "For some time now the situation at the nuclear power plant has continued to be a severe one. There has even been the release of some nuclear materials . . ." The newsroom quieted as journalists scribbled in their notebooks. Several people whispered to one another. Kan continued, "Today we announced the reclassification of this incident as Level 7 on the International Nuclear Events Scale."

The newsroom erupted with questions. "Please. Please," Kan raised his hand. "The situation at each reactor at Fukushima Dai-Ichi Nuclear Power Plant is one moving toward stability." But he could tell he had lost the room. The news was surely already hitting the Internet.

He finished his speech by announcing his hope that people near the nuclear plant would soon be able to return home, and reminding the public that Japan had rebuilt itself before, and he knew it would be able to do it again.

"I pledge here and now in front of the entire nation to continue to give my all to Japan in order to overcome

the earthquake and subsequent nuclear incidents and rebuild our country in such a way as to make it even better than before. I believe we can do this."

Months after the tsunami, some cities, such as Ishinomaki in Miyagi Prefecture, still struggled to deal with damage from the disaster.

PICKING UP
THE PIECES

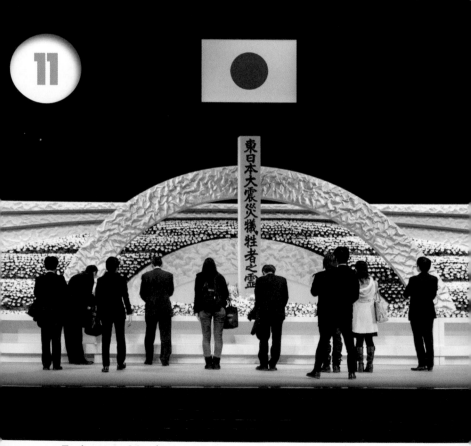

東日本大震災犠牲者之霊

Each year on March 11, many Japanese people pay their respects
to the victims of the 2011 tsunami.

Leticia Morales

Seattle, Washington,
September 8, 2011

It was a beautiful day in Seattle. Leticia Morales opened up her laptop to check Facebook. She noticed a post from her old ship's captain, Thom Burke. Instantly, memories of the time she spent in Operation Tomodachi came flooding back.

The destruction Morales witnessed during those weeks was impossible to forget. She had flown helicopter missions to and from the mainland, bringing supplies to the desperate victims of the earthquake and tsunami. She and the crew were wary of the nuclear plant nearby, but trusted all of the messages they received from Captain Burke that everything was safe. One day, she remembered, Captain Burke had urgently announced that everyone on board must immediately stop drinking tap water and stop showering. Even this news hadn't worried her. *The Navy would never put us in danger,* she remembered thinking.

She smiled when she started reading Captain Burke's post to the crew of the USS *Ronald Reagan*: "We have the pride that comes with superbly conducting one of the most complex humanitarian relief operations in history. . . . Not only did we work through debris fields, cold and icing conditions, but we did not waver amidst an uncertain radiological threat. . . . We overcame our fear and we did our job superbly. Tomodachi was the highlight."

The smile fell from Morales' lips.

What did Captain Burke mean by "an uncertain radiological threat"?

Masao Yoshida

Control Room, Fukushima Dai-Ichi,
December 9, 2011

Masao Yoshida had been retired for exactly eight days before he walked back into the control room at Fukushima Dai-Ichi. He wanted to be the one to inform his former colleagues about his recent diagnosis of esophageal cancer. He knew everyone would jump to the conclusion that it was caused by radiation exposure and he wanted to stop this rumor before it started. He had always been a heavy smoker, and in his mind, there was no doubt that cigarettes were the cause of his disease.

Even though he didn't blame the company for his cancer, Yoshida had mixed feelings about how TEPCO had handled the disaster. He also wondered how much he had contributed to the problems himself. He had even briefly toyed with the idea of starting a business to teach people about the effects of radiation exposure. He had gone so far as to come up with an idea for a name: the Japan Association of

Nuclear Escapers, or JANE for short. The name was a pun. "Jaa-ne" in Japanese meant "goodbye."

As expected, his team was sad to hear the news of his disease. They all wished him well and told him not to worry about things at the plant. They would take care of it, they promised.

Yoshida assured them he would be back to visit in the spring. In his typical fatherly fashion, he reminded everyone to watch the weather: "It is going to get colder. Please take care of yourselves and your families and don't catch a cold."

With that, he bowed deeply, and left the room.

Masao Yoshida

EPILOGUE

The earthquake that struck off the coast of northeastern Japan on March 11, 2011, lasted between three and five minutes and registered at a shocking magnitude of 9.0 on the Richter scale. Known as the Tohoku earthquake, experts now understand that it was the strongest earthquake to hit this region in recorded history. It was so powerful that it moved the entire island of Honshu approximately 8 feet to one side, and shifted the Earth on its axis.

Shortly after the quake hit, a series of gigantic waves rushed toward Japan's coast at speeds close to 500 miles per hour. This is about the cruising speed for jetliner airplanes. One particularly powerful wave traveled 6 miles inland. Eyewitnesses reported seeing waves ranging from 30 to 60 feet tall. Workers at the Fukushima Dai-Ichi plant noticed watermarks on the nuclear plant's exterior that ranged from 46 to 49 feet above sea level.

More than 19,000 people were killed in the earthquake and tsunami, including three TEPCO workers at the Dai-Ni and Dai-Ichi nuclear plants. More than 300,000 people lost their homes as a result of the disaster. Hundreds of aftershocks rocked the already damaged region in the weeks and months after the quake. Though most of these were small, some were as powerful as 7.7 and 7.9 on the Richter scale.

The accident at the Fukushima Dai-Ichi nuclear power plant was the second most severe in history, following the Chernobyl nuclear plant accident in 1986. Workers remain at the plant to this day, continuing their efforts to clean spilled radioactive materials. They are also collecting and storing radioactive water from the area. Using an elaborate filtration process, workers are removing radiation from the stored water. In 2015, the first batch of the filtered water was dumped back into the ocean. Today, there are still about 700,000 tons of radioactive water in storage tanks at the Fukushima Dai-Ichi plant. The subject of what to do with them remains very controversial.

The coast of Minamisoma, Japan, before (top), during (middle), and after (bottom) the 2011 tsunami.

All of the reactors reached cold shutdown status in 2011. This meant that they were cool enough to prevent the release of more radiation. Even so, work will continue at the plant for decades to come. Experts estimate that it will take 30 to 40 years to completely decommission the plant and remove all of the radioactive materials there. Though a small number of residents were allowed to return to their homes in the evacuation zones shortly after the accident, the majority are still displaced. Government estimates report that by 2021, most displaced residents will be able to safely return home.

In the wake of the Fukushima accident, Japan shut down all of its active nuclear power plants to establish better safety standards in order to prevent another accident elsewhere. In 2015, Japan allowed select nuclear plants to resume producing power under new safety guidelines, despite opposition from the majority of the populace.

Though the Fukushima plant released dangerous amounts of radiation, no deaths have yet been attributed to radiation poisoning. More than 40,000 people have worked to clean up the nuclear plant since the accident. Of this group, a small number have developed cancers that may have been caused by radiation exposure. However, the cause of cancers is difficult to pinpoint. While some are influenced by environmental factors, such as radiation, others occur randomly, or due to genetic dispositions. In 2015, the Japanese government agreed to pay for the treatment of one worker's leukemia, agreeing that it was likely caused by his time cleaning up the plant in 2012 and 2013.

Masao Yoshida retired early from his job at the Fukushima Dai-Ichi plant in 2011 when he was diagnosed with esophageal cancer. He died in 2013 from his illness. Upon hearing the news of Yoshida's death, former Prime Minister Naoto Kan tweeted, "I bow deeply out of respect for his leadership and decisiveness." Yoshida is remembered as a hero for his refusal to abandon his post, despite the danger it presented. Yoshida and the other workers who remained at the plant after its evacuation became known as the "Fukushima 50" after the media mistakenly reported that a group of 50 workers had stayed at the plant to keep it from melting down.

This group became famous for their heroism, but were also subjected to criticism for their role in contributing to the disaster.

In the months following the disaster, Naoto Kan became increasingly outspoken against the use of nuclear power. The public and media harshly criticized Kan for not showing enough leadership during the disaster. On September 2, 2011, Kan resigned from his post as prime minister. Today he is an advocate for renewable energy.

Takashi Sato no longer works for TEPCO. He is one of the few Fukushima 50 to speak publicly about his experiences inside the plant.

Atsufumi Yoshizawa continued to work under dangerous conditions at Fukushima Dai-Ichi for nine months after the disaster. He understands that the public has mixed feelings about him and the other members of the Fukushima 50. He says, "We have two faces. On one hand, we are heroes who risked our lives. On the other, we are employees of TEPCO, who caused the accident."

Katsunobu Sakurai continues to serve as the mayor of Minamisoma. He has worked hard to rebuild his city and is an advocate for renewable energy. He has also expressed great anger about the nuclear disaster and believes that Japan needs to pursue non-nuclear energy options in the future.

Susumi Sugawara spent 20 days following the disaster on his boat, *Sunflower*, ferrying people and supplies back and forth from the mainland to the island of Oshimba. Without his boat, many people on the island would have been left completely cut off.

Leticia Morales began suffering from many mysterious health problems in 2013. After having a tumor removed from her kidney and her thyroid removed, she was diagnosed with breast cancer. Morales suspects these complications may be related to her service on board the USS *Ronald Reagan*. She now wonders if the metallic taste she and her shipmates experienced was related to a plume of toxic radiation from the first hydrogen explosion at the plant. Morales joined a group of 79 veterans to file a $1 billion class action lawsuit against TEPCO for their mismanagement of the nuclear disaster.

Sailors on board the USS *Ronald Reagan* load
humanitarian assistance supplies onto a helicopter
during Operation Tomodachi.

TIMELINE

1967: Construction begins on Fukushima Dai-Ichi Nuclear Power Plant.

2002: Fukushima Dai-Ichi's seawall rebuilt to 18.7 feet.

2008: TEPCO engineers warn that Fukushima Dai-Ichi's seawall is inadequate protection against giant tsunamis.

MARCH 11, 2011

2:46 P.M.: Magnitude 9.0 Tohoku earthquake strikes off the shore of Japan.

3:27 P.M.: Tsunami strikes Fukushima Dai-Ichi.

MARCH 12, 2011, 3:36 P.M.: Hydrogen explosion in reactor 1.

MARCH 13, 2011, 6:22 P.M.: Hydrogen explosion in reactor 3.

MARCH 14, 2011, 11:01 A.M.: Hydrogen explosion in reactor 3.

MARCH 15, 2011

6:00 A.M.: Hydrogen explosion in reactor 2.

7:00 A.M.: The U.S. Navy begins to move ships out of the area after detecting small amounts of airborne radiation.

8:30 A.M.: Most of the staff at Fukushima Dai-Ichi are evacuated. Only a small group, who become known as the Fukushima 50, remain.

8:54 A.M.: Fire breaks out in reactor 4.

MARCH 17, 2011, 9:48 A.M.: Japan's Self-Defense Forces helicopters begin dumping seawater into reactors.

APRIL 11, 2011: Magnitude 6.4 aftershock kills six.

APRIL 12, 2011: Japan's Nuclear Agency raises the crisis from a level 5 event to a level 7.

JUNE 6, 2011: Japan's Nuclear Emergency Response Headquarters finally announces that reactors 1, 2, and 3 at Dai-Ichi experienced full meltdowns.

February 2014: 79 sailors from the USS *Ronald Reagan* file $1 billion class action suit against TEPCO for sicknesses they claim are related to radiation exposure.

September 2015: TEPCO dumps filtered irradiated water back into the ocean.

October 2015: Japanese government agrees to pay for a Fukushima worker's medical bills after deciding that his leukemia may have been caused by radiation exposure at the plant.

GLOSSARY

cancer (KAN-suhr)—a serious disease in which some cells in the body grow faster than normal cells

deploy (di-PLOY)—to move troops into position for military or humanitarian action

epicenter (EP-uh-sent-ur)—the point on Earth's surface directly above the place where an earthquake occurs

humanitarian (hyoo-MAN-uh-TAIR-ee-uhn)—to care about the needs of other people and provide assistance to those in need

irradiate (ihr-RAY-dee-ayt)—to expose something to radiation

magnitude (MAG-nuh-tood)—a measure of the amount of energy released by an earthquake

millisievert (mil-uh-SEE-vuhrt)—the unit used to measure radiation exposure

nuclear fission (NYOO-klee-ur FISH-uhn)—the splitting of the nucleus of an atom, which creates energy

prefecture (PREE-fek-chuhr)—an area into which some countries are divided

Self-Defense Forces (SELF-di-FENSS FORSEZ)—the military forces of Japan

tsunami (tsoo-NAH-mee)—a large, destructive wave caused by an underwater earthquake

uranium (yoo-RAY-nee-uhm)—radioactive element found in pitchblende and used in nuclear power stations

radiation (ray-dee-AY-shuhn)—tiny particles sent out from radioactive materials. High amounts of radiation can be harmful to living things.

CRITICAL THINKING USING THE COMMON CORE

1. Many people are angry with TEPCO for the disaster that occurred at the Fukushima Dai-Ichi plant on March 11, 2011. What factors might the company have been able to prevent? (Integration of Knowledge and Ideas)

2. Why was Prime Minister Naoto Kan frustrated with the workers at TEPCO? (Key Ideas and Details)

3. Ultimately, the disaster at Fukushima Dai-Ichi earned a level 7 nuclear accident title. How did the workers try to control the situation? How did people throughout Japan respond to the crisis? (Craft and Structure)

INTERNET SITES

FactHound offers a safe, fun way to find Internet sites related to this book. All of the sites on FactHound have been researched by our staff.

Here's all you do:
Visit *www.facthound.com*
Type in this code: 9781515736059

FactHound will fetch the best sites for you!

FURTHER READING

Birmingham, Lucy, and David McNeill. *Strong in the Rain: Surviving Japan's Earthquake, Tsunami, and Fukushima Nuclear Disaster.* New York: Palgrave Macmillan, 2012.

Bortz, Fred. *Meltdown! The Nuclear Disaster in Japan and Our Energy Future.* Minneapolis: Twenty-First Century Books, 2012.

Immell, Myra, ed. *Japan's 2011 Natural Disasters and Nuclear Meltdown.* Detroit: Greenhaven Press, 2014.

Woolf, Alex. *Nuclear Disaster.* A World After. Chicago: Heinemann Library, 2014.

SELECTED BIBLIOGRAPHY

"2011 Japan Earthquake-Tsunami Fast Facts." *CNN*. March 14, 2016. http://www.cnn.com/2013/07/17/world/asia/japan-earthquake--tsunami-fast-facts.

Brain, Marshall, and Robert Lamb. "How Nuclear Power Works." *HowStuffWorks*. October 9, 2000. http://science.howstuffworks.com/nuclear-power1.htm

Bricker, Mindy Kay, ed. *The Fukushima Daiichi Nuclear Power Station Disaster: Investigating the Myth and Reality*. New York: Earthscan from Routledge, 2014.

Hatamura, Yotaro. *The 2011 Fukushima Nuclear Power Plant Accident: How and Why It Happened*. Cambridge, UK: Woodhead Publishing, 2014.

"Inside Japan's Nuclear Meltdown." *Frontline*. Produced by Dan Edge. February 28, 2012. http://www.pbs.org/wgbh/frontline/film/japans-nuclear-meltdown

Lamb, Robert. "How a Nuclear Meltdown Works." *HowStuffWorks*. April 12, 2011. http://science.howstuffworks.com/nuclear-meltdown2.htm

INDEX

Burke, Thom, 30, 51, 93, 94

control rods, 10, 11

Fukushima Dai-Ichi nuclear plant, 5, 6, 9, 11, 13, 18, 27, 35, 39, 46, 50, 52, 56, 64, 67, 68, 73, 74, 79, 86, 90, 95

Hokaido, Japan, 49
Honshu, Japan, 5, 98

International Nuclear Events Scale, 89, 90

Kan, Naoto, 34–36, 38–42, 46, 49–50, 67–68, 72–74, 87, 102–103
Kesennuma, Japan, 49

Madarame, Haruki, 42–43
Minamisoma, Japan, 14, 24, 79
Morales, Leticia, 29–31, 47–48, 51–52, 93–94, 104

nuclear fission, 10, 11

Okinawa, Japan, 49
Operation Tomodachi, 47, 93
Oshima, Japan, 21

Sakurai, Katsunobu, 14, 24–25, 79–81, 103
Sato, Takashi, 32, 57–58, 63, 103
Sendai, Japan, 49
Sugawara, Susumu, 21, 104
Sunflower, 23–24, 104

Tokyo Electric Power Company (TEPCO), 13, 35, 36, 38, 39, 46, 50, 76, 80, 82, 83, 86, 95, 99, 103, 104

Yoshida, Masao, 4–7, 16, 28, 39–41, 45–47, 55–57, 59, 61–62, 63, 69, 75–76, 95–96
Yoshizawa, Atsufumi, 9–13, 16, 18, 27–29, 64–65, 69, 71, 84–86

ABOUT THE AUTHOR

Rebecca Rissman is a nonfiction author and editor. She has written more than 200 books about history, science, and art. Her book *Shapes in Sports* earned a starred review from *Booklist*, and her series *Animal Spikes and Spines* received *Learning Magazine*'s 2013 Teachers' Choice for Children's Books. She lives in Chicago, Illinois, with her husband and two daughters. She enjoys hiking, yoga, and cooking.